MÁRCIA DE LUCA • LÚCIA BARROS

let's play yoga!

HOW TO GROW CALM LIKE A MOUNTAIN, STRONG LIKE A WARRIOR, AND JOYFUL LIKE THE SUN

FOR KIDS AGES 5 TO 8

illustrations by
Bruna Assis Brasil

translation by
Ana Ban

THE EXPERIMENT

CANCELLED

LET'S PLAY YOGA!: *How to Grow Calm Like a Mountain, Strong Like a Warrior, and Joyful Like the Sun*
Text copyright © 2014 by Lúcia Barros and Márcia De Luca
Illustrations copyright © 2014 by Bruna Assis Brasil
Translation copyright © 2018 The Experiment, LLC

Originally published in Brazil as *Vamos Brincar de Estátua? Ioga para crianças* by Companhia das Letrinhas in 2014.
First published in North America by The Experiment, LLC, in 2018.

The Experiment, LLC • 220 East 23rd Street, Suite 600 • New York, NY 10010-4658 • theexperimentpublishing.com

This book contains the opinions and ideas of its author. It is sold with the understanding that the author and publisher are not engaged in rendering medical, health, or any other kind of personal professional services in the book. The author and publisher specifically disclaim all responsibility for any liability, loss, or risk—personal or otherwise—that is incurred as a consequence, directly or indirectly, of the use and application of any of the contents of this book.

The Experiment's books are available at special discounts when purchased in bulk for premiums and sales promotions as well as for fundraising or educational use. For details, contact us at info@theexperimentpublishing.com.

Library of Congress Cataloging-in-Publication Data

Names: De Luca, Márcia, author. | Barros, Lúcia, author. | Brasil, Bruna
  Assis, illustrator.
Title: Let's play yoga! : how to grow calm like a mountain, strong like a
  warrior, and joyful like the sun / Marcia de Luca, Lucia Barros ;
  illustrations by Bruna Assis Brasil ; translation by Ana Ban.
Other titles: Vamos brincar de estatua English
Description: New York : The Experiment, LLC, 2018. | Audience: Age 5-8. |
  "Originally published in Brazil as Vamos Brincar de Estatua: Ioga para
  crianças by Companhia das Letrinhas in 2014."
Identifiers: LCCN 2018016703 (print) | LCCN 2018017347 (ebook) | ISBN
  9781615195114 (ebook) | ISBN 9781615194933 (cloth)
Subjects: LCSH: Yoga--Juvenile literature.
Classification: LCC RJ133.7 (ebook) | LCC RJ133.7 .D4513 2018 (print) | DDC
  613.7/046083--dc23
LC record available at https://lccn.loc.gov/2018016703

ISBN 978-1-61519-493-3
Ebook ISBN 978-1-61519-511-4

Translation by Ana Ban
Graphic design by Erica de Carvalho
Photos by Fabio Heizenreder
Photo retouch by M Gallego • Studio de Artes Gráficas

Manufactured in China
First printing August 2018
10 9 8 7 6 5 4 3 2 1

We thank the collaboration of the kid yogis pictured in this book (listed by order of appearance): Alice Schwarcz Ligabue, Thiago de Barros MacFarland, Laura Helen de Barros Gurney, Isabela De Luca Auriemo, Henrique De Luca Auriemo, Rachel Ashley de Barros Gurney, Maria Isabel Schwarcz Ligabue, Isabel Maciel de Paula Leite, João Pedro de Luca Auriemo, Fernando Ferreira Souza, and Lívia De Luca Almeida.

ACKNOWLEDGMENTS

I thank my beloved daughters, Ana Paula and Ana Luisa, for giving me the wonderful opportunity of being a grandmother of four gorgeous grandchildren: Livia, Henrique, João Pedro, and Isabela. I also thank Isabel and Fernando, who posed for the photos in this book. And my friends Regina Shakti, who shared my desire to write a yoga book for kids; and Rohit Mittar, for encouraging me to spread Indian culture to Western children.

– Márcia De Luca

I trust, I surrender, I accept, and I am thankful—for everything and everyone in my life. Particularly, I thank my daughters, Laura and Rachel, who make me a better person with each passing day; my grandmother, Lourdes; my mother, Vera; and my sister, Silvia—all of them inspiring women. I am thankful to my father, who still lives in me. To my beloved, my companion in life and in dreams, Richard. To our editors who embraced this project. And to you, who will practice yoga with us!

– Lúcia Barros

"We do not inherit the earth from our ancestors; we borrow it from our children." – Native American saying

CONTENTS

INTRODUCTION

Once upon a time, there was a very cool kid.

Her name? The same as yours! Her looks? Just like yours! She was a very happy kid! As well as being strong, she was healthy and smart.

Her secret was to play every day for a few minutes. However, she wasn't playing any old game! It was a sequence called *yoga*. The name for the game is short and easy to remember, but it also has a beautiful meaning: "union."

Have you ever heard someone saying that together we are stronger? That's what union is! A good example of this is when we gather together our friends to take up a challenge—because three people are much stronger than just one! With yoga, it is the same thing: It brings together our bodies, our feelings, and our thoughts. And then, day by day, we become healthier, stronger, happier, and also smarter.

Do you want to play? Then you must know you will have to dive deep into this game. For example, there is a pose called *mountain*; if you are going to do this pose, your feet must seem stuck to the ground, your spine must be very straight, and your thoughts . . . ah, leave your thoughts aside! Focus on feeling that you are indeed a mountain!

Are you ready? Let's play!

THE RULES FOR PLAYING YOGA

When we start a new game, we first learn how to play, right? This is what we're going to do now. The rules of yoga can be summarized in ten fundamental principles that benefit our lives as a whole, because they teach us about the things we must avoid (*yamas*) and about the things we must try to do more (*niyamas*).

Each principle has a name in Sanskrit, which was the language spoken by the teachers who created yoga more than five thousand years ago. You will see the Sanskrit names here—in parenthesis, under each principle—so you can practice using and saying them.

When we respect and follow these rules, we get stronger on the inside and outside so that we become better, happier people.

Let's get to know the rules!

Nonviolence

(*AHIMSA*)

There's nothing good about any kind of violence. We're talking about physical violence—like what happens when we have a fight—but also thoughts, words, and actions that hurt other people, nature, or ourselves.

Meaning

In life: Treat others only the way you'd want them to treat you; respect and care for animals and plants; treat yourself with the same kindness, patience, and joy that you treat your best friend. The love you must nurture for yourself is called *self-esteem*, and it is key to making your dreams come true, to having good relationships with everyone around you, and to being happy!

While playing yoga: Respect your body and your emotions. Don't practice the moves when you are sick, with a full belly, if something hurts you or makes you uncomfortable or may cause you to get hurt somehow (for example, when you don't use your yoga mat, which we will discuss later).

Truth

(SATYA)

We must always tell the truth and live correctly. Sometimes this is hard: like when we do something wrong and we want to hide what we did or blame someone else. This is not being truthful! We need to be honest about everything we do, even when we have done something bad.

Meaning

In life: Say exactly what you think and feel, and tell the truth about what you do. Did you break the vase in the living room? You must tell your parents! Everybody is going to a party but you'd rather stay home and rest? Tell them you don't want to go! Honesty is important in your relationship with others, but you must always be honest with yourself as well.

While playing yoga: Always try to do your best in the postures, but still respect your body and how it feels today. You can't touch the ground without bending your back? It's fine, just stop when you feel you can't go further! While you're there, focus all your thoughts and efforts and you'll see that with every passing day, you will stretch a little more.

(*ASTEYA*)

Being someone who does not steal can come up in many different situations. It can mean not stealing other people's things, but also their thoughts, words, and actions. You can also not steal from yourself by being honest about what you want and need and what makes you happy. It affects your own life and the lives of everyone around you.

For example, do not say that your friend's idea for a school project or a game is your own; keep your promises; do not do something you know is wrong just because "everybody is doing it," which would be stealing from yourself what you really believe to be right. Instead, show others how good it feels to not do things that are wrong—like gossiping, not sharing your toys, or littering, which prevents others from enjoying a clean and safe environment. Be a beautiful example of sharing.

Take seriously the pose you're doing, paying attention to the game so you respect your body and mind's focus and energy. In that moment, feel that you are really a mountain, a tree, or a warrior—some of the poses we will do together later in this book.

Right Use of Energy

(BRAHMACHARYA)

Using energy in the right way is one of the most important rules for playing yoga and in your life. It helps you overcome challenges because you learn to spend your energy practicing something right, according to the rules, every day and with focus, even when you'd rather be lying down doing nothing! This makes everything you do more fun, and you feel the effects more strongly in your body and mind.

Meaning

In life Have strength of character so that you won't choose one path just because it seems easier, and devote yourself to whatever you're doing like there's nothing more important in the whole world. That might mean doing your homework when it's time instead of playing video games, because working hard at school will make you smart; or saying no to more cake if you feel full, even if it's very tasty; or seeing that you already have lots of toys instead of buying a new one; or trying to calm yourself down when you're fighting with a friend instead of yelling at him. You have to follow your school and your family's rules, even when there's no one looking, because that will teach you to do the right thing no matter what.

While playing yoga Even if your arms or legs start to get tired, try to stay in a pose with a lot of focus. Try to play at least twice a week (every day is even better!), always focused and breathing, and you'll see that it will be easier to do the poses every time.

Detachment

(*APARIGRAHA*)

No one needs too much of anything—toys, clothes, food, and other things—to live well and be happy. It is very important to learn to share all the good things we have, which means that we'll all need fewer new things of our own. Have you ever heard that humans are consuming more natural resources, like clean water and food, than Earth is capable of giving us? Detachment has everything to do with the idea of a more sustainable world, in which we only use what we need without harming others or the environment.

Meaning

In life: Stop and think when you feel like you want something very badly for yourself and ask if you really need it. Being jealous of what other people have, or holding on to things you don't need, won't make you have more fun or be happier. Instead, you can share with others by donating clothes you don't want anymore or that don't fit you, or toys you don't play with anymore. Always offer to help others, even if it means getting less for yourself. Eat just enough so you're not hungry, drink just enough so you're not thirsty.

While playing yoga: Let go of feeling like you have to be perfect all the time. For example: In this book you will see someone doing the Elastic pose and touching his feet with his hands . . . But if when you do the pose you can only reach your knees, no problem! Give it your best—your best is always enough.

Cleanliness

(*SAUCHA*)

We must take care of our body, our homes, our towns, nature, the animals, the whole planet. Cleanliness can also refer to having thoughts and feelings that are clear, sincere, and kind, rather than hurtful or dishonest.

Meaning

In life: Take care of your own body by brushing your teeth and washing with just the necessary amount of water and soap. Take care of your room and your whole house, putting whatever you use back where you found it and helping to clean and organize even if someone else made a mess. Respect nature and all other living beings including animals, bugs, and plants. Never litter on the beach, on the grass, or in the ocean or rivers. Have positive thoughts and feelings, cleansing your mind of bad or angry ideas.

While playing yoga: Take care of the place where you're going to play so it's clean and airy. Carefully store your yoga mat and clothes so you can use them for a long time. Do the poses correctly and follow the rules without cheating.

Contentment

(*SANTOSHA*)

Being content means being happy with your life, choosing to be joyful, and looking at the good things the world offers you every day. Life does not have to be hard—although you do have some responsibilities, it can be fun and easy if you are content.

Meaning

In life: Wake up in a good mood, happy for the day ahead, and try to smile even when things are difficult and you feel like you have a problem. Choose happy and joyful words when you talk to your friends, parents, and siblings. One practice that might help bring more contentment into your life is to write down three things that made you joyful that day, every night before bed. This teaches you to see all the good things life brings you.

While playing yoga: Be happy with your efforts, because no matter what you are taking care of your health and of your mind when you play.

Discipline
(TAPAS)

No more laziness! In order to do what you want to do every day, you need focus and persistence even when things are hard. At the same time, you also need to rest, or just distract yourself by playing a little, so you can replenish your energies. We have to work hard, but it's important not to be too easy or too strict with yourself.

Meaning

In life: Try to do things on time and in the right order every day: getting up in the morning, doing your homework before watching TV or playing video games, eating your healthy dinner before dessert. Always give your best when learning new things and making new friends.

While playing yoga: Try to do the poses even when you think they're hard, to practice even when you don't feel like it, and to try to stay in the poses a little longer every day.

Self-Study

(SVADHYAYA)

Our bodies send us messages of comfort and discomfort all the time, and we need to learn to listen to them and what they mean. In order to do that, you need to learn to observe everything you feel, even the smallest of things, such as shivering when you're cold or a rumbling in your hungry belly.

Meaning

In life: Every day, spend a few minutes being quiet, paying attention to your body and your emotions. Try not to think of them as "good" or "bad," but just watch them. Make the connection between a feeling of fear and a pain (for instance, in your stomach), or check if you feel more energized in your body when you are happy about something.

While playing yoga: Be totally focused in what you're doing so that you know how much you can do before you hurt yourself. Be aware of every inch of your body, from your little toe to the top of your head, so that you can feel good and supported in the pose the whole time.

Trust

(ISHVARA PRANIDHANA)

Have you ever heard anyone say that, in the end, everything will be all right? It means that things happen in their own time. Trusting is a kind of wisdom that gets deeper as you get older. Not everything happens the way we wanted, but we can feel okay about it as long as we did our best.

Meaning

In life: Trust in yourself, in your ability to learn and to overcome your challenges, more and more and even when you're not sure you can do it. Maybe math is hard for you, and you get frustrated with your homework. Pay attention in class, study a little more, and believe you will improve. You should also not be afraid to ask for help: Trust your parents and your teachers.

While playing yoga: Whenever you practice a pose believe you can do it to your best ability, even if it's hard at first. You will see that the more you play, the easier everything gets!

LET'S PLAY YOGA!

WHERE, WHEN, HOW, AND WHY

In yoga, the poses we do are called *asanas*. This is a word that comes from Sanskrit, the language of the first yoga teachers we mentioned in the beginning of this book.

Just like anything we do in life for the first time, it's a good idea to start slow! You can read the stories and instructions a few times, and the more you play and learn, the longer you will be able to stay in each pose.

WHERE

You can play yoga in your room, in a corner in the living room, outside . . . The main thing is that the chosen place must be clean and airy. Always make sure you have your yoga mat—it is rubbery so you won't slip in the poses and get hurt.

WHEN

The best times to play are early in the morning or at the end of the afternoon. Don't play when your stomach is full after eating or when you're sick.

HOW

Play barefoot, wearing clothes that are comfortable and not too loose. In this game, we always try to combine movement and breath. Usually, we breathe in when we move upward, and we breathe out when we move downward, with the air moving in and out through the nose rather than the mouth. In each pose, pay attention to how your body breathes in and out. Your breath should be very calm and slow, not nervous or fast. Breathing this way helps us to concentrate better and relax, so we can get stronger and stay in the poses longer.

Be careful trying out the poses so you don't hurt yourself. The idea is to do everything safely and comfortably, right? If you feel any pain while doing any movement, stop and talk to an adult so they can help you.

WHY

Remember the poses called *asanas*? They bring many cool things. You feel healthier, stronger, and have more balance and flexibility when you practice them. They also help you to be more focused, so that it's easier to learn, study, and achieve the things you want. Practicing can seem difficult on your body sometimes, but you'll see that it also makes you calm—really calm—especially when you breathe slowly and deeply.

So this game is good for your body, your mind, and your feelings!

LET'S BREATHE!

Now you will learn the right way to breathe—not only while you're playing yoga, but during the rest of the day, too.

Lie down on your back and bend your knees. Put your hands on your belly. Breathe in deeply through your nose, sipping in the air until you feel completely full in your lungs and your belly. While you breathe in, imagine that little light flecks, like gold glitter, are coming into your body. Imagine you are a balloon filled with that glitter. Now breathe out through your nose, slowly letting the air go as if your balloon was losing its air, until you feel that your chest and your belly are empty. You can feel your breathing with your hands on your belly: It goes up and down as the air comes in and goes out.

It may feel strange to breathe this way at first. But if you practice, it will soon become so natural that you won't need to think about it anymore.

Here's a great tip: Before a test at school, when you feel upset or worried, or when you have to make an important decision, stop and breathe deeply. Imagine the glitter balloon inflating inside your body. Do that a few times to calm yourself, and then go ahead!

TADA THE MOUNTAIN

(*TADASANA/MOUNTAIN POSE*)

ONCE UPON A TIME . . .

. . . there was a mountain called Tada. It was high, sturdy, impressive, and majestic—just like a king or a queen.

One day, strong—really, really strong—winds started to blow. They howled like wolves and shook everything in their path: trees, flowers, leaves, bushes . . . The closer they got to the town, the more everybody trembled. But not Tada, who stayed comfortably fixed to the ground, its peak almost touching the sky.

The winds kept blowing against the mountain with all their strength . . . And still it didn't move.

"Wow, this mountain is strong!" they thought. So they blew and blew and blew until they got very tired. They slowed down until they were breezes and began to fall asleep. And still Tada stayed in place: unshakable, majestic, firm, and strong.

NOW IT'S YOUR TURN . . .

You, too, can be like Tada the mountain: steady, calm, and unmoveable in any situation—at home, at school, or when you are with your friends.

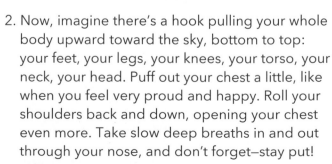

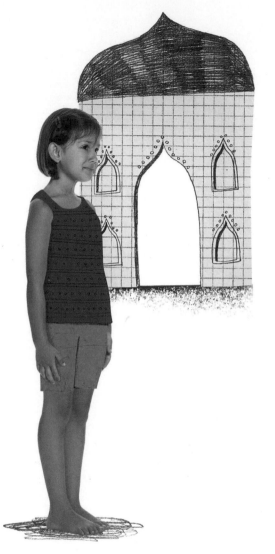

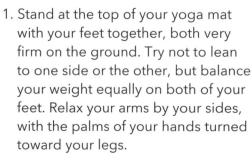

1. Stand at the top of your yoga mat with your feet together, both very firm on the ground. Try not to lean to one side or the other, but balance your weight equally on both of your feet. Relax your arms by your sides, with the palms of your hands turned toward your legs.

2. Now, imagine there's a hook pulling your whole body upward toward the sky, bottom to top: your feet, your legs, your knees, your torso, your neck, your head. Puff out your chest a little, like when you feel very proud and happy. Roll your shoulders back and down, opening your chest even more. Take slow deep breaths in and out through your nose, and don't forget—stay put!

Think of Tada's qualities.
You have those same qualities:
You're firm, strong, unbeatable.

WHY PLAY AT BEING TADA?

- Your posture improves: upright and tall, not slouched.

- Your focus increases: The whole time, you only think about being more like Tada the mountain.

- And you can use what you have learned here in many different situations of your life!

3. That's it! Now you are Tada the mountain. Keep paying attention to your breathing while you stand tall and strong.

VRIKSHA THE TREE

(*VRIKSHASANA/TREE POSE*)

ONCE UPON A TIME . . .

. . . there was a magic tree called Vriksha. It gave people anything they wanted—all they had to do was ask. Everyone was good to each other. They shared what they had and treated each other with respect.

As time went by, some people started wanting more and more, much more than they needed. They also stopped sharing the things they had with their friends and neighbors. Vriksha was sad when it saw this happening. It was so sad it decided to move.

It was chaos! People came looking for the magic tree and couldn't find it. Some people were angry. Some people wept.

Little by little, men, women, and children came to realize that the world was better when everybody received and shared like Vriksha. People also found out that having lots of things didn't make anyone happier. Happiness is having just enough of what we need—including good friends!

Vriksha was so moved when it saw people changing their minds that it decided to come back home, to the place in the town where it stood before.

Don't you think the trees where you live are a little magic as well, like Vriksha? They bloom flowers and create shade; they are home to birds and other animals; and, above all, their roots hold the soil all around us in place. Take good care of them, and they will take care of you!

31

You, too, can be like Vriksha the magic tree. Its strong roots allow you to hold on to and be loyal to the things you believe in and want—for yourself and everyone you know. In being like Vriksha, you share all the good things you have: your friendship, your love, your gifts.

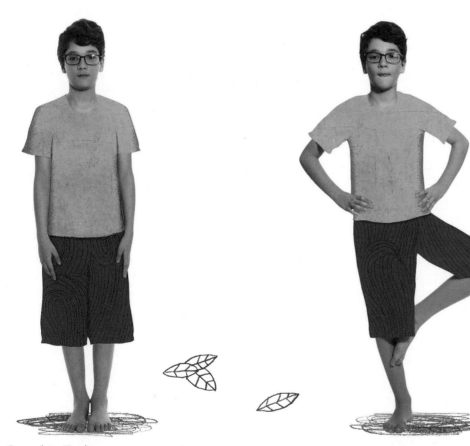

1. Stand in Tadasana, mountain pose.

2. Put your hands on your hips. Now, bend your left knee up into the air and place the bottom of your left foot on the inside of your right leg, above or below your knee (but not on your knee).

3. Breathe in deeply and bring your arms high above your head. Touch your palms together like you are praying.

Think of the qualities of Vriksha.
You have them all: firm character,
strength, and the ability to share.

WHY PLAY AT BEING VRIKSHA?

- Your balance and your focus improve.

- And you can use what you have learned here in many different situations of your life!

4. That's it! Now you are Vriksha the tree. When you're ready, put your left foot down and stand again in Tadasana, mountain pose. Repeat everything using the other side of your body, remembering to breathe in and out the whole time.

TRIKO THE TRIANGLE

(TRIKONASANA/TRIANGLE POSE)

ONCE UPON A TIME . . .

. . . there was a triangle called Triko. Its three sides were all the same size, perfectly balanced. It didn't matter how strong the wind, rain, or sun were, Triko was always at ease.

One day, the animals in the forest got together to go talk to Triko. They wanted to know its secret. Triko smiled, happy to be able to share its wisdom. It always went straight to the point, never round and round in circles or back and forth in a zigzag. It would say exactly what needed to be said, and would do exactly what needed to be done.

So Triko showed the animals its secret. The side that was responsible for its physical shape, the side that was responsible for its thoughts, and the side that took care of its feelings—they were all the same. No one side was larger, or stronger, or better.

"All of you can be balanced just like me," Triko said.

"But how?" asked the animals.

"You have to play yoga!" Triko answered. "And little by little, you, too, will be able to experience the feeling of living in perfect balance."

Isn't that easy? Why don't we try?

NOW IT'S YOUR TURN . . .

You, too, can be like Triko the triangle: balanced in your body, your emotions, and your thoughts. When these three parts of you are in harmony, you'll feel healthy and happy.

1. Stand in Tadasana, mountain pose.

2. Jump to separate your legs wide apart and your arms out to the sides. Keep your palms facing down.

3. Turn your whole left leg completely to the left side of your yoga mat. Turn your right foot in to the left a little bit as well, with your toes facing the front right corner of your mat Breathe in, and reach your left arm up and your right arm down, making a diagonal line Look up at your left hand.

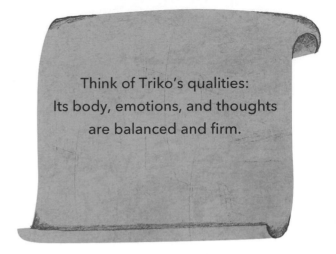

Think of Triko's qualities:
Its body, emotions, and thoughts
are balanced and firm.

WHY PLAY AT BEING TRIKO?

- Your feet, ankles, and legs get stronger.

- Your chest opens.

- Your back muscles get stronger.

- Your thoughts and your emotions are at ease while you focus on your fingers.

- **You can use what you have learned here in many different situations of your life!**

4. As you breathe out, keep your back tall and bend your body over to the left until your hand touches your leg, your ankle, or the floor outside your foot. Reach your right arm straight up to the sky, and gently turn your head to gaze at the tips of your fingers—but don't hurt your neck.

5. That's it! Now you are Triko the triangle. Breathe in, stand up straight again, and lower your arms. When you breathe out, jump your feet back together to stand in Tadasana, mountain pose. Then, repeat the steps on the other side.

VIRA THE WARRIOR

(VIRABHADRASANA II/WARRIOR II POSE)

ONCE UPON A TIME . . .

. . . there was a warrior named Vira. He was the best soldier in his town: the most courageous and the wisest. Everybody admired him and wanted to be just like him.

Vira, however, had a secret: In his room, there was a mirror where another warrior lived. He looked like Vira but didn't act like him: He was very selfish and a cheater. But Vira was not afraid of the warrior in the mirror and faced him every day with respect.

One morning, Vira woke up hearing cries for help. He realized the voice was coming from the mirror. When Vira looked, the warrior inside looked sick.

"I feel so bad, Vira, but no one will help me," he said. "Break the mirror, please! Come to my rescue."

Vira then understood why he had to live with the mirror-warrior. He was trying to trap Vira, to bring him to the dark side of the mirror. He realized that his reflection was showing him another side of himself, since they were both the same, but that he had to choose to be well instead of sick—to act right instead of wrong.

Vira faced the mirror feeling stronger after meeting his darker side. He acted with even more courage and wisdom, treating others only the way he'd want to be treated.

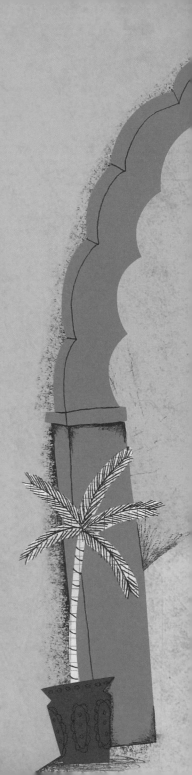

NOW IT'S YOUR TURN . . .

You, too, can be like Vira the warrior: strong, brave, and righteous. Just like him, we all have a mirror inside ourselves: It shows us the thoughts and actions that we know to be wrong, but that are there nonetheless. Just like Vira, however, you can control that side and learn from it. Practicing warrior pose is how you become a better person with each passing day.

1. Stand in Tadasana, mountain pose.

2. Jump to separate your legs wide apart and your arms out to the sides. Turn your palms to face down.

3. Turn your whole left leg and turn your right toes a little to the left, like in triangle pose. Then bend your left leg, but keep your right leg straight. Look over your left hand at your fingertips, but keep your torso facing forward.

40

4. Breathe in as you raise your arms up and join your palms in a prayer above your head. Turn your gaze to face forward again.

5. That's it! Now you are Vira the warrior. Straighten your left leg, turn your body to the front, and jump your feet together to stand again in mountain pose. Repeat everything on the other side.

Think of Vira's qualities:
You're courageous, strong, and fair.

WHY PLAY AT BEING VIRA?

- Your energy increases.

- Your lungs expand and your chest opens.

- Your legs, shoulders, and back muscles get stronger.

- Your mind settles and you feel powerful and sure of the right way, just like Vira.

- And you can use what you have learned here in many different situations of your life!

PASCHIMO THE ELASTIC

(PASCHIMOTTANASANA/SEATED FORWARD BEND)

ONCE UPON A TIME . . .

. . . there was an elastic called Paschimo. It was humble and small but strong and thick. One day, it was invited to take part in a competition in the forest.

The first event of the competition was to jump up high and touch a branch of a tree. All the animals stood in line waiting for their turn. Paschimottana was the last one. No one thought that the small elastic would be able to come close to the branch. However, it started to stretch and stretch and stretch . . . And soon enough it stretched so far it touched the branch! It wasn't just any branch, either, but the highest branch of the tree. Paschimo won the game!

Paschimo kept surprising the other animals all during the competition with its stretchiness—it could get longer and shorter, and thin enough to slide under narrow spaces no one else could fit through. It was so flexible it could accomplish any task presented—all because it could adapt to each and every different situation.

NOW IT'S YOUR TURN . . .

You, too, can be as flexible as Paschimo the elastic and adapt to life's challenges, both in school and at home. Flexibility is one of the most important qualities for our well-being. With it, everything gets lighter and easier.

1. Sit down with your legs straight in front of you and close together, with the tips of your toes pointing upward, your back straight, and your arms next to your sides.

2. Breathe in, raise your arms up, and interlace your fingers like a web. Turn your hands inside out so your palms face the sky. Straighten your arms . . . Stretch them as much as you can, as if you were an elastic.

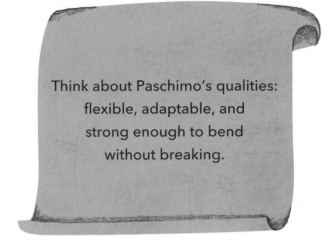

Think about Paschimo's qualities: flexible, adaptable, and strong enough to bend without breaking.

WHY PLAY AT BEING PASCHIMO?

o Your insides will be stronger and your heart will be peaceful.

o There will be more blood in your brain, energizing your mind.

o Your thoughts will get quieter while you stretch and focus on being like the elastic.

o And you can use what you have learned here in many different situations of your life!

3. When you breathe out, release your hands and bend your body over your legs until you can touch your toes or any part of your legs, stretching as much as you can without it hurting. In this pose, breathe in and out with no hurry and stay like this for a little while.

4. That's it! Now you are Paschimo the elastic.

USTRA THE CAMEL

(USTRASANA/CAMEL POSE)

ONCE UPON A TIME . . .

. . . there was a camel called Ustra. He was tall and thin and lived in a city just outside a vast desert. When the king got sick, Ustra was called to the palace. The king asked him to go fetch a doctor who lived very far away on the other end of the desert.

"You're the only one who can make this journey," said the king to the camel.

It was true: The other animals would try to explore the desert, but because there was no water, they couldn't go far. They could only go near small areas in the desert called oases, where water pooled into little lakes. But Ustra could go long distances in the desert thanks to the two humps on his back that stashed water.

Ustra started out on his journey and quickly returned with the doctor for the king. When he went to sleep that night, his dreams were peaceful—he felt good knowing that being prepared could help others.

NOW IT'S YOUR TURN . . .

You, too, can be like Ustra the camel, who always has enough extra energy to go where he wants.

1. Kneel down with your legs slightly separated and the tops of your feet on the floor, toes pointing to the back of your yoga mat. Press your shins and the tops of your feet against the ground so you can reach the top of your head higher toward the sky.

2. Breathe in deeply and raise your arms up, stretching your sides all the way.

3. Breathe out and tip your body backward, bringing your head and shoulders back and in the direction of your feet. Keep your chin and eyes looking up, so your neck stays long while you stretch. Open your chest while you breathe in and bend, going down slowly. If you can, rest your hands on your heels; if not, bring your hands to your waist.

4. That's it! Now you are Ustra the camel. Breathe out to lift yourself back up, bringing your hands, one by one, onto your hips. Return to the starting pose on your shins and breathe deeply with your eyes closed.

In this pose, think of Ustra's characteristics. You have the same qualities, as you carry within you your own store of energy to face any journey.

WHY PLAY AT BEING USTRA?

○ Your posture improves as your back and shoulders get stronger but also more relaxed when you bend.

○ Your focus increases and your mind relaxes, knowing that you have extra energy inside yourself for when you need it.

○ And you can use what you have learned here in many different situations of your life!

GOMU THE SPOTTED COW
(*GOMUKHASANA /COW FACE POSE*)

ONCE UPON A TIME . . .

. . . there was a cow named Gomu. She would wake up with the rising sun and sleep as it set. Gomu spent her days calmly grazing on the grass in the fields.

One day, a woman sat down in the field next to Gomu. She looked very tired. Having grown up on the farm, she had known Gomu since she was a girl, and now that they were both older she wanted to talk to her friend.

The woman grew more tired as she told Gomu about her troubles with her fidgety son, who was also visiting the farm during his vacation from school. He couldn't sit still and always had a stomachache. He wouldn't finish his dinner or his homework, and every night he went to bed so late he couldn't wake up in time for school. He wouldn't listen to her or his dad. And he always wanted to do the opposite of what the other kids did for fun: He wanted to swim in winter but wrap himself up in blankets in summer.

Gomu, who was also a mother to a baby cow, stopped grazing to answer her friend. She asked the woman to bring the boy to her field and spend a day with her.

The next morning, when the sun was rising, the boy was taken to Gomu. She gave him a game to play: He was challenged to mimic anything she did as well as he could.

All that day, the boy followed the cow and the flow of the nature: He played when it was time to play, he ate when it was time to eat, he rested when it was time to rest. He loved that day and felt so good! Gone was his stomachache, and he was so hungry he ate all his dinner plus a little more. When evening fell, he went to bed; the next day, he got up with the sun, and with Gomu. When his mom came to bring him home, she smiled to see her fidgety son so calm and happy. She thanked Gomu, who sent her a loving moo back.

NOW IT'S YOUR TURN . . .

You, too, can be like Gomu the spotted cow, who follows nature's rhythms, is healthy, and has ease in her heart.

1. Sit down on your yoga mat and cross your legs, so your right knee is on top of your left knee. Breathe deeply with your back straight.

2. Breathe in and raise your left arm up. Bend your right arm and draw it behind your back. Bring your hand behind you, and try to touch the middle of your back with your fingers.

3. Bend your left arm, so your elbow points up to the sky, and try to bring your hand to touch your back. Crawl the fingers of your right hand up your back until they meet your left hand. Hook your fingers. Press your bottom down into the floor, and breathe in to stretch your spine and open your chest.

In this pose, think about Gomu's qualities: good health, ease of heart, stability, peace. You also have these same qualities.

4. That's it! Now you are Gomu the spotted cow. Let go of your hands and uncross your legs to come back to sitting easily on your mat. Then repeat everything on the other side.

WHY PLAY AT BEING GOMU?

- Your posture improves: straight back, open chest, shoulders aligned.

- Your legs become stronger, preventing a restless feeling when you sit.

- Your mind understands that you're part of nature.

- And you can use what you have learned here in many different situations of your life!

SETU THE BRIDGE

(*SETU BANDHA SARVANGASANA/BRIDGE POSE*)

ONCE UPON A TIME . . .

. . . there was a bridge called Setu that connected two sides of the town. Two kids lived on one side of the bridge, and their school was on the other side. One day, when it had rained too much, everything was flooded—the streets, the houses, and Setu. When the kids arrived at the bridge to go to school, they couldn't see Setu at all.

That day, then, the kids couldn't go to school. They didn't see their friends, and they didn't learn anything with their teacher. They were sad when they went to bed that night because they hadn't liked being by themselves all day.

The next day, the sun was shining brightly and the floods were drying up. Setu reappeared and called the kids over to cross it so they could go to school. They were so happy to not be alone they didn't even realize when it got dark. Setu had to call them to come back home for dinner.

"But we want to stay here," they said.

"I'm sorry, my friends," replied Setu. "But there's a right time for everything: time to play, time to rest, time to study, time to eat. Time to get wet, and time to be dry. Now, it's time for you to go back home."

The kids listened to Setu and when they got to their bedrooms, they felt a different kind of happy: being cozy at home. They thanked Setu the bridge for the lesson that day.

NOW IT'S YOUR TURN . . .

You, too, can be like Setu the bridge, capable of connecting our homes to the rest of the world, where we can meet and play with other people: the world of friends, school, neighbors, and families. When we cross between these two places on a sturdy bridge, we can feel balanced and happy to know we're not alone.

1. Lie down on your back. Bend your legs and place your feet flat on the ground with a little space between your legs. Leave your arms loose by your sides and relax your neck.

2. Breathe in, push your feet into the ground, and lift your body and hips while you squeeze your buttocks. Use your arms to press down into your mat and lift up higher. Interlace your fingers like a web behind your back on the floor and balance your body's weight between your shoulders and your feet. Breathe deeply and open your chest.

3. That's it! Now you are Setu the bridge. Stay in this pose for a few moments, and when you're ready release your hands and lower back down to the floor. Breathe in and out.

WHY PLAY AT BEING SETU?

- You strengthen your legs, hips, and back.

- You breathe more deeply with your chest open toward the sky.

- Your mind focuses on the comforting knowledge that you can play but also go back home any time you want.

- And you can use what you have learned here in many different situations of your life!

MATSYENDRA THE TEACHER

(MATSYENDRASANA/WISE MAN POSE)

ONCE UPON A TIME . . .

. . . there was a wise old teacher called Matsyendra. He knew everything and was able to solve any problem. All you had to do was come to him with your question. But getting there was very hard because he lived deep inside the forest. There were many distractions along the way, so it was easy to get lost and have to go back home without even seeing Matsyendra.

This is what happened the first time a young girl tried to find the wise teacher. She was very messy and wanted to learn how to better clean up after herself. Her mother explained which way she should go, and she set off very early in the morning. However, when she got to the forest, she was excited by everything she saw and started to play. Before she knew it, it was dark and already time to go back home.

The next day, her mother sent her out again. Again the little girl got distracted by all there was to see and play with.

She tried again for a third time, but now much more determined: Today was the day she would meet the wise teacher, no matter what. After much walking, and trying hard not to play, she got to Matsyendra's house. He welcomed the little girl with a smile. He was very old and his voice was low and quiet. If she didn't pay close attention, she wouldn't be able to hear his lessons.

The little girl explained her problem: She was too messy! Her room had too many toys and things and her mom would get upset at her. She asked what to do.

"You already know what you have to do," he replied. "The same thing you did in order to get here."

And then the little girl understood: In order to solve her problems, she needed concentration, to not get distracted, and to ask those who know more than she for help.

You, too, can be like Matsyendra the teacher,
who is always calm, focused, and knows the answers
to any question or problem.

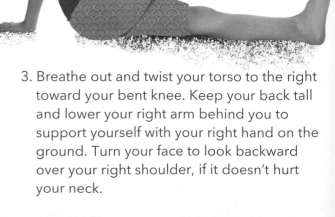

1. Sit down on your yoga mat with your legs stretched in front of you and your back tall. Breathe in deeply and raise your arms, lengthening your sides up to your fingertips.

2. Bend your right leg and cross your right foot over your left leg, keeping your foot close to your hip. Stretch your left leg long with your toes pointing upward. Breathe in and bend your left arm to hold the outside of your right knee.

3. Breathe out and twist your torso to the right toward your bent knee. Keep your back tall and lower your right arm behind you to support yourself with your right hand on the ground. Turn your face to look backward over your right shoulder, if it doesn't hurt your neck.

Stay in the pose for a few moments, thinking about Matsyendra's qualities: calm, focus, concentration. You, too, can develop these qualities!

4. That's it! Now you are Matsyendra the teacher. Uncross your arms and legs to return to the starting pose. Breathe in and out and repeat the same sequence on the other side.

WHY PLAY AT BEING MATSYENDRA?

- With a long trunk, your spine will feel strong but flexible.

- The organs inside your torso—your liver, gallbladder, and pancreas—are energized so they can work well to digest your food.

- Your mind learns to be quiet and focused so that you can listen to the messages of the wise teacher who exists inside of you.

- And you can use what you have learned here in many different situations of your life!

SIMHA THE LION

(SIMHASANA / LION'S BREATH)

ONCE UPON A TIME . . .

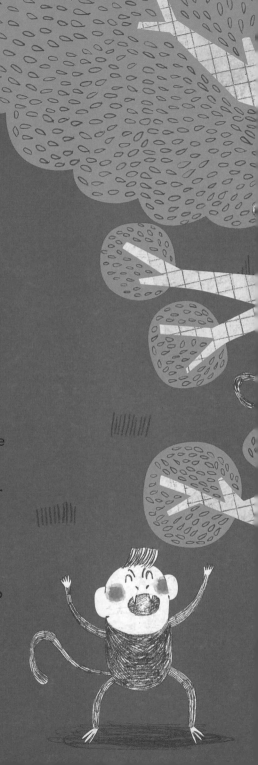

. . . there was a lion called Simha. He was the king of the forest and known all around for being fair. The animals lived in peace, until one day the monkeys started a fight.

The other animals couldn't understand what was happening: Every morning, the monkeys would tell a different story about why they were fighting. Soon everyone was upset by all the fighting about fighting. The animals went to speak to Simha, and he called the monkeys to his cave at sunset to talk about their problems.

Simha was ready to meet the monkeys, but hours went by—no one showed up! Distracted by their fighting, they forgot they had to go see the king. When Simha was tired of waiting, he made the whole forest tremble with a mighty roar. In the many years he had been king, he had never needed to use his voice in that way, but he knew that power inside him would make a difference.

The monkeys came to him right away. Simha calmed down and asked them why they were fighting. All the monkeys started to answer at the same time, and Simha realized the problem: They couldn't understand each other because they weren't listening!

With another roar, the lion made everyone quiet down. He told the monkeys they had to listen to one another if they wanted their fight to end. Simha explained how important listening is to getting along.

Slowly, each monkey explained his wishes, fears, and point of view to the others. The other monkeys listened carefully and made an effort to understand each other. Their fighting stopped, and the forest was peaceful once again.

NOW IT'S YOUR TURN . . .

You, too, can be like Simha the lion, who listens well to others and makes his words clearly heard by all.

1. Kneel down and tuck your toes under your feet on the ground. Rest your buttocks on your heels and sit with your back tall.

2. Lean your body a little forward, but keeping your back long. Open your hands next to your shoulders as if they were big lion's paws.

3. Breathe in deeply, and when you breathe out, make a face like a lion: eyes and mouth open wide. Stick your tongue out and ROAR!

While you make this pose, think of Simha's qualities: fairness, clear thinking, good communication, ability to listen and understand. You, too, possess these qualities.

4. That's it! Now you are Simha the lion.

WHY PLAY AT BEING SIMHA?

○ You open your mouth wide so you can breathe deeper and fuller.

○ Your voice is strong and firm.

○ Your thoughts and the way you express yourself are clearer.

○ And you can use what you have learned here in many different situations of your life!

SURYA THE SUN

(SURYA NAMASKAR/SUN SALUTATIONS)

ONCE UPON A TIME . . .

. . . there was a sun called Surya who shone brightly in the sky. Full of energy and life, he commanded the heavens. He cast his light on everyone and on all the paths down on Earth. And all the planets in space lived happily around him, too.

Until one day, clouds came and covered the sun. At first, it was just a little bit. But then they blocked Surya's light completely.

The planets didn't like that at all! Without Surya, it was very cold and everybody was sad, wanting to do nothing but sleep like it was nighttime. The planets were so concerned they decided to get together to ask the wind to help them.

The wind that blew that day was the strongest there ever was. It blew and blew, until all the clouds were gone.

Surya reappeared, strong and bright as ever. His energy, warmth, and light spread through the whole sky and made the planets happy once again.

NOW IT'S YOUR TURN . . .

You, too, can be like Surya the sun, full of energy and capable of illuminating everyone around him with his kindness. The sun game is actually a sequence of movements that feels best in the morning because it makes you full of energy—for school or for playing—for the day ahead. If you can, do this sequence twice in a row.

1. Stand with your back tall, your feet close together, and your palms joined at the center of your chest. Breathe in fully, and breathe out deeply.

2. The second time you breathe in, lift your arms up overhead. Stretch your arms straight up, like you were trying to reach the sky.

6. When you breathe in, stretch your arms so you can bring your head and chest up off the floor. Keep your feet, legs, and hips down, and try not to let your shoulders touch your ears. Breathe out and open your chest from the center to your shoulders. Move your shoulders back toward your feet—but be careful not to hurt your neck and your spine.

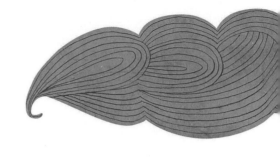

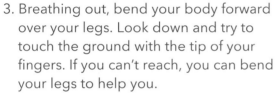

3. Breathing out, bend your body forward over your legs. Look down and try to touch the ground with the tip of your fingers. If you can't reach, you can bend your legs to help you.

4. Bring your hands all the way to touch the floor. Breathe in, look ahead, breathe out and step your feet straight back so your legs are long like a plank.

5. Rest your knees on the floor and bend your arms to slowly lower your whole body onto the ground. Control your descent with the strength of your arms.

7. Breathing in, rest your knees on the floor. Breathe out and lift your hips up, making a table shape with your body. Then stretch your legs straight, forming a triangle shape with your hands and feet on the ground and hips high up toward the sky. Breathe in, trying to make your back and legs longer.

8. When you breathe out again, press strongly into your hands and jump or step your feet to the top of your yoga mat so they land between your hands in a crouched position. Breathe in, straighten your legs and lift your chest. Breathe out and refold over your legs, as if you were trying to kiss your own knees.

9. Breathe in and come back to standing up straight, lifting your arms straight up to the sky. When you breathe out, release your arms next to you and move your shoulders a little back so you can open your chest, as if the light of the sun was shining out from your heart.

10. That's it! Now you are Surya the sun. Breathe in and go back to the starting pose, with your hands joined at the center of your chest. Repeat the whole thing a second time if you can.

WHY PLAY AT BEING SURYA?

- Your whole body gets to move: Your spine, your abdomen, your legs, and your arms all get stronger and more flexible.

- You create energy to fuel all your activities during the day, like the sun fuels the plants and people on Earth.

- Your ability to focus increases.

- And you can use what you have learned here in many different situations of your life!

THE SUPER RELAXER

(YOGA NIDRA)

After all this playing, you deserve a rest! The best part is that, when you relax after yoga, you will have found inside you a few superpowers: focus, intelligence, courage, health, strength, flexibility, joy—and knowing you have the power to do anything good you want to do!

Relaxing is always important, and not only after you play. Life cannot be all about studying or doing your tasks and chores at home. Remember: You also need time to quiet your mind and your heart in order to have balance.

So let's stop talking and let's start relaxing!

First, let's relax your mind with a simple breathing exercise:

- Sit down comfortably with your legs crossed and your back very straight. Rest your hands on your legs with your palms face up.

- Bring your right hand to your face and lightly press your right nostril with your right thumb as you breathe in through the left nostril.

- Holding the breath in, move your hand to the other side of your nose and use the thumb to press your left nostril as you breathe out through the right nostril.

- Keep the left nostril pressed and breathe in through your right nostril.

- Switch sides again: Press your right nostril with your right thumb and breathe out through the left nostril.

This is one full cycle of relaxing breathing, which you can repeat as many times as needed when you want to calm down or regain focus.

Next, let's relax your whole body:

- Lie down comfortably on your yoga mat or a soft blanket. Relax your arms by your sides, with your palms turned up and your feet and ankles relaxed, probably falling a bit out to the sides.

- Close your eyes and start to go through each part of your body in your mind. Start with your feet and go up to your head, gradually relaxing each little part along the way.

- Now, try counting backward from ten. By the time you get to one, you are completely relaxed!

- Stay like this for a few moments, quiet and not thinking of anything in particular, without controlling your breath, just enjoying being still, just resting . . .

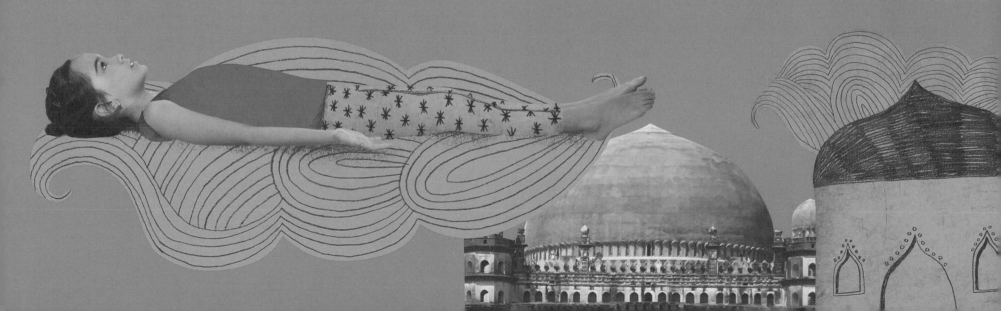

MEDITATION

THE MAGIC WORD

Sometimes our thoughts are so busy it feels like there are monkeys jumping around inside our heads! They want everything at once, they can't stop talking, they're fighting and talking all the time. Just like Simha the lion was able to calm them down with clear communication, there is a magic word you can use to quiet the monkeys in your head: *om*.

To practice saying the word *om* requires some attention like the yoga poses. Begin by sitting comfortably on the floor with your legs crossed and your back tall. Rest your hands on your legs and touch your thumb to your index finger. Close your eyes and mentally repeat *om*, *om*, *om*, with a long *m* sound like a buzzing bee. Do this for a few minutes, and you will see how those monkeys quiet down!

Of course, while you're trying to focus, you will think of other things. You might feel an itch you want to scratch, a little hungry, or ready to drift off to sleep. Do you know who is responsible for those distracting thoughts and feelings? All those monkeys! However, little by little, as you repeat the magic word *om*, you will calm the monkeys to be perfectly silent. Won't that feel great?

Try to use this word every day, not only when your mind is very restless. You will see that with time, you feel will happier and happier!

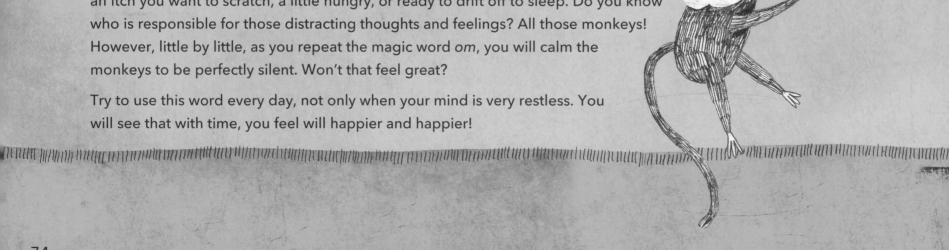

HOW TO PLAY YOGA WITH YOUR KIDS FOR A BETTER, STRONGER, AND MORE BEAUTIFUL LIFE

A GUIDE FOR PARENTS FROM THE AUTHORS

A healthy body, more focus and creativity, more flexible muscles and ideas, a better quality of life—in short, greater well-being. These are some of the benefits of yoga, and a great gift we can give to our children!

Everybody, adults and children, suffers from stress, busy lives, and competition. From early on, little ones may not even have time to play since their schedules are as full as their parents'. We may be teaching our children to always want and need to do more, and live on autopilot. This prevents them from having fun, being curious, and knowing their true essence.

Connecting to our true essence is the key to understanding the endless possibilities of our lives. By training body and mind at the same time, and giving us a solid base of values, yoga helps us realize the pure potential we're all born with. It restores our original, balanced state and brings us back in contact with our deepest selves, where our absolute creativity resides. When we are free to imagine with a clear mind and steady breath, we can (re)invent ourselves in any way we want.

Yoga also reconnects us to each other to build a better world together. With today's crisis of values, our sense of duty, community, and kindness seem to have been lost. The importance of intentional living seems to have been replaced by the need to own more things, and then to show them off on social media and on our phones.

Taking all of this into account, we believe that the mission of parents and guardians is to help children stay connected to their essence. This way they can truly find their purpose in life (their *dharma*, in yoga philosophy) and then use this aim not only to benefit themselves but all humanity. This is the path to happiness according to the teachings of yoga.

Frequent yoga practice contributes greatly to this aim: Its principles include nonviolence (toward yourself and others), discipline, effort, detachment, and others that reveal the power within each and every one of us. Gradually, children will learn that they can find comfort and the answers to all their questions right inside themselves rather than from others or possessions.

In other words, yoga gives us roots at the same time it teaches us how to fly.

Wherever we direct our focus and attention is where we place the power of our potential. Is there anything you want, for yourself or others? Don't just dream it, go and get it! Did you make a mistake? Start again! Is something hard? Practice and breathe, and it will be easier tomorrow. And don't forget to always smile at your efforts. These are some of the ways kids will learn through yoga to trust themselves to do good in the world.

But that's not all, because yoga will also improve your kids' health. Regular yoga practice helps regulate the respiratory and digestive systems, balance hormones, lower blood pressure and cholesterol levels, improve sleep patterns, boost immunity, and elongate and strengthen muscles. It is extremely effective at preventing and healing diseases such as hypertension, diabetes, asthma, obesity, high cholesterol, hormonal imbalances, digestive issues, and back pain.

We believe our children do not belong to us. They choose us to be their parents every step during their difficult task of growing up. It is with our example that we teach them to follow the right and true path.

Thus, here is our invitation to you: Add yoga values to your life and practice the poses with your kids. You all will live happily—and healthfully—ever after!

– Márcia and Lúcia

ABOUT THE AUTHORS

I am a mother and a grandmother and I have been studying yoga, meditation, and Ayurveda for almost forty years. I have traveled to India and the USA many times and studied with different American and Indian masters. I see an urgent need for us to teach children how to meditate and live a life connected to the highest values, so that together we can all build a better world. Playing yoga is such a teaching, and in the process children have a lot of fun!

Márcia De Luca

(with her grandchildren Lívia, Isabela, João Pedro, and Henrique)

I am a mother, a teacher, and a journalist. I have been studying yoga and meditation for over twenty years and, since my daughters were born ten years ago, I have also been researching and writing on the science of happiness. Márcia and I have written three books together and we are partners at Bindu Escola de Valores (Bindu School of Values), where we teach mindfulness at schools and companies. For more information, follow us on Instagram @binduescoladevalores or check our website binduescoladevalores.com.br.

Lúcia Barros

(with her daughters Laura and Rachel)

ABOUT THE ILLUSTRATOR

As a kid I would spend hours in bookshops. I loved to create my own stories, especially the drawings. Even though I studied journalism and design in school, I only started illustrating as my job after I graduated. I traveled to Barcelona for special studies, and here I am now, illustrating all kinds of books. Today I jump from one story to the next, imagining a new world each day. If you want to see some of my other work, visit my website www.brunaassisbrasil.com.br.

Bruna Assis Brasil